VOWS, VOWELS, AND CONSONANTS

A COLLECTIONS OF POEMS

SWARN VERMA

To my family,
for your love that grounds me.

To my friends,
for your laughter that lights the way.

And to the quite force behind these words ,
who taught me the true depth of love.

This book is for all of you,
for shaping the words within these pages.

Contents

Acknowledgements — *vii*

Author's Note — *ix*

1. Rising In Love — 1

2. Endless Kindness — 5

3. Wings Of Hope — 7

4. The Love Letter — 11

5. Tides Of Devotion — 14

6. Feathers Of Freedom — 18

7. Curse Of God — 23

8. The Moon And The Star — 27

9. Cretaceous Love Story — 31

10. Butterflies — 35

11. War For Love — 38

12. Unanswered Hearts — 41

13. The Swan — 46

14. Extraterrestrial Love — 49

15. The Greatest Language — 52

16. Love Of The Heavens — 57

17. Promises — 60

18. The Loveless World — 64

19. Healing Force — 70

20. Why Agent Of Love ? — 76

Acknowledgements

First, I thank God, whose grace and wisdom have been my guiding light throughout this journey.

To my family, your unwavering love and support have been my foundation. This book is a reflection of your strength and belief in me.

To my friends, thank you for being my constant cheerleaders, for lifting me through doubts, and for celebrating every small victory.

Thank you to everyone who has walked alongside me in this journey.

Author's Note

"*Poetry has a way of capturing emotions that mere words often fail to express. This book is a collection of moments—some lived, some imagined, and some felt so deeply that they refused to be forgotten. Each poem stands on its own, yet they are all bound by the most powerful emotion of all - love.*

Love in its many forms—its longing, its warmth, its ache, and its quiet miracles—runs through these verses like a thread; weaving together scattered thoughts and unspoken feelings. These poems are not just mine; they belong to anyone who has ever searched for meaning in silence, found comfort in a memory, or carried a story too precious to be told aloud.

There is no single way to read this book. Read it as a lover, a dreamer, or simply as someone passing through. If even one line lingers with you, finds a home in your heart, or feels as if it was written just for you—then these pages have served their purpose."

1. Rising in Love

They say, falling in love,

as if love were a descent,

a fragile thing, prone to cracks and shatters,

a tumble from grace into chaos,

an accident waiting to happen.

But tell me,

when has anything that falls

not ended up broken?

Why do we tether love

to the pull of gravity,

to a force so mundane, so ordinary?

Love is not an anchor;

it is the wings we didn't know we had,

the lift that defies all weight,

the ascent that makes us

more than we thought we could be.

Imagine this—

standing on the edge of your own doubts,

your own insecurities,

and instead of falling,

you rise.

Rise to where the clouds cradle your dreams,

to where the air hums with possibilities,
to where love feels like sunlight
warming every corner of your soul.
If what you call love
pushes you down,
if it fills you with dread instead of light,
then pause.
Look at the cracks forming in your heart,
the weight you've been told to carry,
and ask yourself:
Is this love,
or a storm disguised as shelter?
True love doesn't demand you shrink.
It doesn't leave you gasping for air,
clawing to hold on to something
that slips through your fingers like sand.
True love stands beside you and says,
Let's rise together.
Rise-
to where the stars seem within reach,
and every glance feels like the first,
where flaws are not flaws
but patterns in the tapestry of who you are.

Rise—
to where love isn't a possession,
but a state of being.

Rise—
to where jealousy evaporates like morning mist,
and all that remains is devotion,
pure and steady like a flame
that never wavers.
If you've fallen before,
if your heart still aches from the impact,
know this:
falling was never the way.
Love was never meant to bruise.
Reconsider, reset.
Strip away the illusions,
and find the love that calls you higher.
Because when you rise in love,
you see the world differently.
The noise fades.
The bitterness dissolves.
And all that's left is clarity,
the breathtaking truth
that love was never a fall.
For love is not the ground beneath you;
it is the sky above,
the stars that guide,
the wind that carries.
And when you rise in love,
you are not just in love.

You are love.

2. Endless Kindness

It was a strange sight to see someone
Taking his frogs for a walk.
At first, I thought, What a crazy guy.
But as I looked closer,
Something stirred within me,
A thought that reached deep inside,
Making me pause and wonder about him.
Upon closer inspection,
I saw those tiny frogs were tied with a string—
Not tight enough to trap them,
But loose enough to keep them close.
It wasn't the first time someone must've stopped,
But I bet most would've missed what I noticed.
Love, often called the most powerful force,
Is not about caging the one you love,
Nor is it about letting them wander free.
It's about finding balance—
Giving freedom, while holding hands.
It's like flying a kite to the moon,
But never losing touch with the earth,
Because once that touch is gone,
The kite can no longer fly.

The smile on that kid's face,
Radiating satisfaction and joy,
At the thought of taking care
Of his tiny best friends,
Makes me wonder,
How easily love and happiness can be spread.
Yet, we're often lost in our own perception,
Making love seem like the hardest thing to do.
When those frogs were leaving for their next destination,
One of them stopped to say a final goodbye
To that kid.
Maybe it was with sadness, or perhaps just a regret
Of not being able to stay with him longer.
But those tiny eyes of the frog held a message for the boy,
A message it wanted to share with the world.
A message that, if followed, could bring peace to the land,
A message strong enough to shatter hate.
In the eyes of that frog, there was a feeling of pride,
Pride in having stayed with such a gentle soul.
In the eyes of that frog, there was gratitude,
Gratitude for showing kindness to a speechless creature.
And in the eyes of that frog, there was a silent request—
A request to carry this kindness throughout his life.

3. Wings of Hope

I sit by the window,
the sun hiding in the horizon,
and I commanded the wind :
"Carry them gently, my two white pigeons,
born of dreams and feathered with hope."
One for love,
the other for peace,
I send them forth,
to touch a world that has forgotten
the softness of kindness,
the rhythm of hearts in harmony.
They rise, their wings brushing the morning sky,
light as airs , strong as prayers.
A mapless journey,
guided not by stars, but by something purer—
the pulse of yearning humanity.
Through bustling cities,
where the weight of ambition
bends even the tallest skyscrapers,
they glide unseen.
Their wings sweep over the gray streets,
leaving trails of invisible warmth

in hearts too cold to recognise it.
They pass children with empty hands
and fill them with unseen happiness.
They perch on crumbling walls
that divide us,
and whisper into the cracks,
"You are not stone; you are hope waiting to grow."
Through forests,
where the silence of trees listens intently,
they rest on branches heavy with dew,
sharing tales of a world
trying to heal.
In war zones,
they dodge the deafening screams of hatred,
their feathers untouched by blood.
Instead, they sing—softly,
like lullabies in forgotten tongues—
until even soldiers pause
to remember a mother's kiss,
a child's laugh,
a lover's promise.
Across deserts,
they fly through the searing winds,
their shadows fleeting over endless sands.
They bring cool whispers to cracked lips
and remind the earth
that life, like love,

always finds a way to bloom.
They visit the lonely,
the weary,
the lost.
To the woman crying in her kitchen,
to the old man staring at an empty chair,
to the boy who hides his scars—
they carry tiny sparks of light,
just enough to remind them
they are not alone.
And when they return,
their wings are heavy with stories,
their feathers kissed by every corner of the world.
I hold them close,
and they tell me:
"The world still aches,
but in its cracks,
we left seeds.
And from those seeds,
one day,
gardens will grow."
So I said to the wind again:
"Fly, my pigeons,
fly once more.
For love is not a single act—
it is a journey,
and the world needs it endlessly."

And the pigeons take flight,
their wings shimmering in the dusk,
carrying with them
all that we hope for
but cannot hold.

4. The Love Letter

Folded in her trembling hands,
the parchment carried her heart—
ink smudged with the weight of unspoken words,
her love poured between each line.
She sealed it with hope,
with a kiss of his name,
and sent it across the winds of war.
He received it under a sky
painted in fire and ash.
The battlefield paused,
just for a moment,
as his hands, calloused by battle,
gently unfolded the paper.
Her words were soft,
like a lullaby to his tired body.
She spoke of the life they dreamed of—
a cottage by the river,
their children's laughter carrying veggies in the baskets,
her love waiting for him like the dawn.
His lips curled into a fragile smile,
the kind that belongs to a man
who has seen too much darkness

but still dares to believe in light.
Her words became his armour,
a shield against the chaos,
a promise that there was more to life
than the clash of swords and the cries of the fallen.
But fate is cruel.
A whistle through the air—
a single bullet,
piercing his chest before her words could fully sink in.
His hand clenched the letter
as he fell to the earth,
her love pressed to his heart
like a final hug.
He bled,
but it was not the wound that hurt most.
It was the thought
of the letter she'd never receive,
the reply he'd never send,
the dreams they'd built
now left to crumble.
The battlefield grew still around him,
his brothers-in-arms unaware
of the love story ending
in that fleeting moment.
His breath faded,
but her words stayed with him,
etched into his soul

like the memory of her voice.
Far away, she waited,
her heart tethered to the hope
of his return.
But the wind carried no reply,
only the silence of loss,
and a grief that would bloom in her chest
like a flower that refuses to wilt.
Her letter reached him,
but his love carried it back to her—
in the whispers of the wind,
in the glow of the stars,
in the silence that spoke louder than words.

5. Tides of Devotion

Long ago, before the tides had a rhythm,
and the sand knew the weight of waves,
the beach and the ocean existed,
side by side,
but strangers to each other.
The ocean was wild, untamed,
wandering the world with no direction,
its heart brimming with stories of distant lands,
but no one to share them with.
The beach, quiet and steady,
watched from afar,
its grains sparkling under the sun,
waiting for someone
to notice its still beauty.
One fateful dawn,
as the first light kissed the horizon,
a wave, shy and uncertain,
grazed the edge of the beach.
And for the first time,
they felt each other—
a spark, a hum,
a connection that neither could deny.

The ocean marvelled at the beach's calm,
its ability to remain unshaken
despite the world's chaos.
And the beach, oh, the beach fell in love
with the ocean's depth,
its boundless energy,
its stories that carried the weight of the world.
Day after day,
the ocean came closer,
sending wave after wave,
trying to understand the beach.
And the beach stood steady,
letting the ocean pour its heart out,
listening with the kind of patience
only love could inspire.
But soon, they realised a cruel truth—
they could never be one.
The ocean's depth was too vast,
too consuming,
and the beach's stillness,
its very essence,
would be lost in the ocean's arms.
To come together would mean
to destroy each other,
and neither could bear
the thought of such a loss.

So they wept under the stars,
their sorrow mixing with the tides,
until the moon said to them,
"You cannot unite,
but you can choose to stay."
And so they made a promise.
The ocean vowed to return,
again and again,
to bring its stories, its pain,
its joy, its storms.
It would come not as a conqueror,
but as a lover seeking refuge.
And the beach, steadfast and true,
vowed to always wait,
to listen, to soothe,
to never abandon the ocean,
no matter how wild its waves became.
By day, the ocean would wander,
chasing the horizon,
learning the secrets of the world.
And by night, it would come back,
its waves curling into the beach's embrace,
narrating tales of distant shores
and uncharted depths.
The beach, in turn,
would soak up every word,
holding each story in its grains,

keeping them safe,
never letting them fade.
It found joy in being the ocean's sanctuary,
its quiet haven amidst the chaos.
Their love was not in being one,
but in their devotion—
a love that chose distance over destruction,
presence over possession.
Every tide, every wave,
was a reminder of their promise,
a bond that no storm could break.
And so they remain,
the beach and the ocean,
lovers who cannot unite,
but who will never part.
Theirs is a love that transcends touch,
a love that dances on the edge of eternity,
forever apart,
but always together.

6. Feathers of Freedom

They say, "Be detached, don't care too much,"
and some think it means closing your heart,
shutting the door on feelings,
locking away the things you love.
But that's not detachment—
that's running away.
Imagine a bird, perched on a branch,
its claws gripping tightly,
afraid to let go.
When the storm comes,
the branch breaks,
and the bird falls, unready.
This is the harm of misunderstood detachment—
when we cling too hard or push too far.
Some believe detachment means not loving,
not feeling,
not dreaming too big.
"It's safer this way," they say.
But is it safer?
Or is it emptier,
like a garden without flowers,
or a sky without stars?

Detachment isn't a cold wall
or a chain that holds you back.
It's more like the wind—
soft, steady,
always moving,
never tied to one place,
but touching everything.
True detachment doesn't say,
"Don't care about your friends."
It says,
"Care deeply, but don't control them.
Let them be who they are."
It doesn't whisper,
"Don't love."
It sings,
"Love with all your heart,
but don't lose yourself in it."
It's not about throwing your toys away,
or never playing your favorite game.
It's about knowing
that if one day the toy breaks
or the game ends,
you'll still be okay.
You'll miss it, sure,
but you'll find new joys,
new stories to tell.

*Detachment doesn't mean
you stop feeling sad when things go wrong.
It means you don't let sadness
wrap around you like a blanket forever.
You let it come,
sit with it for a while,
and then let it go,
like a kite released into the wind.
Sometimes, we hold on too tightly—
to people, to things, to ideas.
We say, "This is mine,
and if I lose it, I'll be lost too."
But detachment reminds us,
"Nothing is ever truly ours,
not forever.
The best things in life are borrowed—
the laughter of a friend,
the beauty of a sunset,
even the stories we share."
And if we hold too tight,
we might crush the very things we love.
Like a flower plucked too soon,
or a butterfly trapped in a jar.
Detachment isn't about saying goodbye
to everything you enjoy.
It's about saying hello
to the freedom of not clinging,*

to the joy of loving without fear.
It's sitting with your favorite book,
knowing the last page will come,
and that's okay.
Because the story lives on in your heart,
even after the book is closed.
It's cheering for your team,
even when they lose,
because the game was still worth watching.
It's saying,
"I will try my best,"
without being crushed if things don't go your way.
True detachment is balance—
like riding a bicycle,
not too far left, not too far right.
It's letting life flow,
like a river winding its way,
sometimes fast, sometimes slow,
but always moving forward.
So next time someone says,
"Be detached,"
remember this:
It doesn't mean not caring.
It means caring with an open hand,
not a closed fist.
It means loving the journey,
even when the path changes.

It means finding joy,
even when things are different than you planned.
And it means knowing, deep inside,
that you are strong,
not because you hold on to everything,
but because you can let go
and still be whole.
This is detachment—
not a wall,
but a bridge;
not a void,
but a freedom.
And in that freedom,
you'll find life's greatest treasures.

7. Curse of God

Before the first star knew how to shine,
before the wind knew where to run,
before hearts knew what it meant to break,
he walked among the dust of the unborn world—
a God without a throne, without a name.
He was made of warmth, of longing, of firelight in winter.
His voice carried the weight of soft goodbyes,
of held hands in the dark,
of lips that trembled before they spoke.
He taught the sky how to blush in sunsets,
taught rivers how to chase the ocean,
taught the wind to take names never meant to be forgotten.
He placed longing inside every being,
so they would search for something beyond themselves,
so they would ache and call it beauty.
To the mortals, he gave love—
not as a gift, but as a burden worth carrying.
He showed them how to hold another soul
without crushing it,
how to touch without taking,
how to stay even when the nights became storms.
And in return, they worshipped him,

not with temples,
but with the way their eyes softened
when they saw the ones they loved.
"But the world has never known how to cherish what is given
freely."
And where love grew, so did envy.
A darkness rose—something sharp and hollow,
a being with no name but many faces.
It called love a weakness,
twisted its edges until it looked like chains,
whispered into hearts that power
was safer than passion,
that it was better to own than to hold.
The God of Love stood against it,
barefoot in the middle of a war
where swords clashed, but the real wounds
were in the souls of those who forgot how to feel.
They struck him down.
Not with weapons,
but with the weight of a world
that had turned love into a foolish thing,
a reckless thing,
a thing for the weak.
And as he fell,
his own creation looked away,
ashamed of the ache in their hearts,
ashamed that they still needed him.

But before his light faded,
before his warmth turned to dust,
he cast a final curse upon the ones who thrived in cruelty—
"You may wear crowns and hold kingdoms in your fist,"
"but you will never know peace."
"You will build empires, but you will fear the day they crumble."
"And one day, when the world has forgotten my name,"
"someone will rise—"
"not with weapons, not with wrath,"
"but with love so deep it will shatter your bones."
"And that will be the day you fall."
And so the curse lingers still.
In every tyrant's sleepless nights.
In every ruler who drowns in his own greed.
In every soul who thinks they have conquered all,
only to be undone by the light in another's heart.
And somewhere, in the quiet spaces between heartbeats,
his voice still lives—
in the way a mother hums to her child,
in the way two lovers reach for each other in the dark,
in the way even the loneliest soul still hopes,
still believes,
still waits for a love that will make them whole.
For love is never truly defeated.
It waits.
It endures.
It returns.

And one day,
it will rise again.

8. The Moon and the Star

I was walking down the lane,
when the sky was dark,
and all it had was the moon
and just one single star,
tucked above it,
like a secret held too close,
yet still shining for the world to see.
And I thought—
is this what love looks like?
A vast emptiness,
and yet, you only need one person—
or, in their case,
one moon,
one star.
The moon, calm and composed,
bathing the night in its borrowed glow,
acting like it doesn't care.
But we all know the truth, right?
The moon looks up every chance it gets,
just to check if the star is still there,
watching over it.

And the star—oh, the star—
you'd think it's tiny,
but no,
it's loud in its silence,
a quiet guardian,
a speck of brilliance saying,
"Don't worry, I've got you."
It's funny though, isn't it?
How the star sits so far,
as if the universe itself
is afraid to let them get too close.
But I bet the star doesn't mind.

It's not about the distance, after all—
it's about being the one
the moon looks up to.
And here's the part that gets me:
the moon, despite its grandeur,
still hides its scars,
its craters.
But the star?
It doesn't care.
It loves the moon, flaws and all,
because, let's be honest,
even scars glow
when the right light finds them.

The moon whispers,
"Why do you always stay there, so far,
when you could be anywhere else?"
The star replies softly,
"Because love isn't about closeness;
it's about constancy.
I don't need to touch you
to feel you.
I don't need to be near you
to care for you.
I stay because your light gives me purpose,
and my glow reminds you
you're never alone."
The moon sighs,
"But I'm flawed,
scarred, imperfect.
Why would you choose me?"
The star twinkles,
its voice calm and steady,
"Love isn't about perfection.
It's about seeing the craters
and calling them beautiful.
It's about knowing your shadows
and still choosing to stay."
The moon hesitates,
"But we're so far apart.
Doesn't the distance hurt?"

The star answers,
"Distance doesn't weaken love;
it reveals its strength.
I'm here, above you,
not because I have to be,
but because I want to be.
Even from afar,
I guide you,
as you guide me."
And in the quiet night,
as the dark sky holds them both,
the moon glows a little brighter,
the star twinkles a little longer,
and their silent bond whispers a truth:
love doesn't demand proximity—
it thrives in presence,
in patience,
and in the promise
to always be there.

9. Cretaceous Love Story

You know, I've always wondered—
Is love just a human thing?
Or is it something more,
Something that echoes in the cracks of ancient rocks,
In fossils,
In the silence of the earth's forgotten heartbeats?
So there I was,
Sitting in my palaeontology class,
Chapter title: "Behavioural Patterns of Prehistoric Species."
Yeah, sounds fancy—basically means,
"Let's dig up old bones and make educated guesses!"
And then it hit me.
What if that fossil,
You know, that fossil—
The one where two dinosaurs are lying together, intertwined—
What if that was their famous love story?
Like the Romeo and Juliet of the Late Cretaceous Era?
Maybe they were running from a predator,
And one said, "Go! Save yourself!"
But the other said, "Not without you!"
Cue the dramatic meteor entrance—BOOM.
Love wins. Or…well, nobody wins, technically.

Or maybe,
They were the Jack and Rose of their time.
Except this time, no one had to let go.
The meteor was their iceberg,
And the end credits rolled too soon.
Or maybe they were just two rebels,
Running away from the rules of the herd.
One said, "Let's leave this valley and find our own way,"
And the other followed.
Not because they knew where they were going,
But because they knew who they wanted to go with.
Or, maybe,
They were parents.
And as the earth shook and fire rained down,
They stood their ground,
Shielding their little ones
Until their bodies turned to stone.
Love doesn't always look like roses—it's also sacrifice.
And maybe, just maybe,
They were two old souls,
Too tired of running,
Too tired of fighting the world.
And they made a promise:
"When the end comes,
Let's face it together."
And they did.
And 65 million years later,

Here we are, digging them up,
Trying to piece together their story
Like nosy neighbours collecting gossips through the wall.

And isn't that funny?
We've been searching for love stories in the heavens,
In poems, in music, in movies,
When all along,
The earth itself was holding one close to its chest.
But here's the thing—
If love existed even back then,
Among creatures with teeth bigger than my torso,
Who couldn't swipe right,
Who couldn't write sonnets,
Who couldn't even say, "I love you"…
Then maybe love isn't ours to claim.
Maybe it's something bigger.
Because love isn't about language.
It's more than flowers, or chocolates, or cheesy lines.
It's the unsaid promise of "I'll stay."
Even when the ground shakes.
Even when the meteors fall.
Even when it's the end of the world.
So here's to the dino couple—
The OG lovebirds.
Maybe they didn't mean to teach us anything.
Maybe they just wanted to be together.

But isn't that the greatest lesson of all?
And as I closed that chapter in my palaeontology book,
I thought about how love doesn't die with time.
It finds new forms, new stories,
And it waits patiently to be rediscovered.
I realised—
Love isn't just ours.
It's written in fossils,
Etched in time,
A story that will outlive us all.
Funny, isn't it?
We study bones to learn about survival,
But in the end,
They teach us how to love.
Because in the face of the unimaginable,
Even creatures as ancient as dinosaurs chose love.

10. Butterflies

Butterflies don't walk;
they dance.
Even when the world is silent,
their wings sing—
a soft hum of colours brushing against the wind.
But have you ever watched them closely?
Their flight isn't graceful.
It's chaotic.
They zigzag like they're lost,
like even they don't know where they're going.
...Kind of like us,
chasing dreams we forgot the meaning of.
Their beauty is blinding—
wings dipped in sunsets and rainbows.
But here's the irony:
they'll never see themselves.
No mirrors in the butterfly world,
no Instagram filters for their wings.
Maybe that's why they're free.
They don't need validation;
they exist
simply because they do.

But isn't beauty its own punishment?
To be admired,
to be desired,
to be chased—
until your fragile body is pinned to a board,
labeled and forgotten in some collector's glass case.
We do that too.
To people. To ourselves.
"Be pretty," they say.
"Be bright, be bold, be worth noticing."
But nobody tells us what it costs
to shine.
Butterflies don't have cocoons forever.
That's the deal, right?
You break free,
you bloom,
and then you carry the weight of the world's gaze.
But what they don't tell you
is how heavy wings can feel.
And yet...
maybe that's why they flap so hard—
why they move like the wind owes them rent.
Maybe they're not flying;
they're fighting.
Against gravity. Against time.
Against the inevitable ending of everything beautiful.

And us ?
We're not so different.
We stumble forward,
hearts full of colours no one else can see,
hoping—just hoping—
that our chaos might spark something.
Because isn't that what they say?
A butterfly's wingbeat can move mountains,
can start storms,
can change lives.
Even when it doesn't know.
So, here's to the butterflies—
who don't know their own beauty,
who don't care about their destination,
who remind us, in their fleeting chaos,
that it's not the flight
but the flap
that changes the world.
And maybe...
we're all just butterflies
pretending we know how to fly.

11. War for Love

They say war is destruction,
that it comes with the stench of gunpowder,
with boots crushing the earth beneath them,
with the roar of conquest drowning out the cries of the fallen.
But this war—
this war will not be fought with swords.
No flags will burn.
No rivers will run red.
This is a war where voices rise like thunder,
where silence is shattered like brittle glass,
where chains, unseen for centuries,
snap beneath the weight of truth.
It is a war against fear,
against the shadows that coil around the weak,
against the whispers that say, This is how it has always been.
No more. Not anymore.
It is a war for love,
not the love of two,
but the love of all—
a love that does not kneel before power,
that does not beg for permission to exist.

It is a war for peace,
not the brittle truce built on fear,
but the kind carved into the bones of the earth,
so deep that even time cannot erode it.
It is a war for happiness,
not the fleeting kind dangled like a prize,
but the kind that grows wild and untamed,
that spreads in laughter, in kindness, in fire-lit eyes that refuse to
dim.
It is a war for justice,
not the justice that settles scores,
but the justice that uproots the rot,
that turns old thrones to dust,
that rewrites history with hands unshackled.
This war will not be fought in the shadows.
It will not wait for permission.
It will not retreat.
It is waged in the streets,
in the hearts of the weary,
in the fists that refuse to tighten in anger,
in the minds that refuse to be caged.
It does not break. It does not bend.
It does not end until the last wound has healed,
until the last lie has crumbled,
until the last man, woman, and child can stand unafraid,
under a sky that belongs to all.

This is war.
Not with fire. Not with blood.
But with something stronger—
something that no empire, no tyrant, no history
has ever been able to silence.
This is war.
And we will win.

12. Unanswered Hearts

Everyone dedicates their words to those they've loved—
The ones who filled their voids with stars,
The ones who left, taking pieces of the universe with them.
Some pen odes to one-sided love,
The bittersweet ache of wanting what will never be.
But what about those who loved us?
Not the ones we begged for love from,
Not the ones who broke our hearts—
No.
This one's for those who offered us everything
And asked for nothing back.
It's for you,
The girl with the kind eyes,
Who memorised my coffee order,
And waited for hours just to walk home together.
I saw the way she looked at me,
Like I was something rare.
But I pretended not to notice.
And when I smiled politely and said,
"You're such a great friend,"
I broke something in her
That I never even tried to fix.

It's for her,
The girl who sat across from me in silence,
Her gaze soft,
Hoping I'd look up and see
What she couldn't put into words.
But I never did, did I?
Not because I was blind,
But because I was too afraid
Of the weight of her love.
It's for the stranger
Who sent me anonymous poems—
Each line being a thread of his soul,
And me?
I laughed,
Tucked them away like forgotten receipts,
Never thinking twice
About what it took to write them.
His love,
Unseen.
His words,
Unread.
And how cruel I was,
How selfish—
To bask in the warmth of being loved,
Without ever stepping close enough
To feel its fire.

Oh, we talk about heartbreak, don't we?

The betrayal, the tears,

The sleepless nights spent chasing ghosts.

But what about the guilt?

The quiet, nagging weight

Of knowing someone stood in the rain for you

While you stayed dry.

Of knowing someone's dreams had your name etched in them,

And you walked away,

Not because you had to ,

But because you wanted to .

Because hearts are liars,

And sometimes they just refuse

To beat for the people who deserve them most.

And yet,

They never made me feel guilty.

They never threw their love at my feet

And demanded it be picked up.

No.

They walked away with grace,

Carrying their love

Like a wound they'd never show me.

Hypocrisy, isn't it?

We mourn the ones who didn't love us back,

But never the ones

Whose love we left on the doorstep.

We cry for the hands we couldn't hold,

But what about the hands
We never reached for in the first place?
And now, I wonder—
Where are they?
Did they find someone
Who saw their love for what it was—
A gift,
Not a burden?
Did someone hold them
The way I never could?
I hope they did.
Because they deserved more than me,
More than the hollow echoes of my apologies.
And me?
I carry them with me still,
Not as regrets,
But as lessons.
As whispers that remind me:
"The greatest cruelty
Is not breaking a heart you love.
It's breaking a heart
You never even tried to hold."
So here's to you—
The ones I let go
Because I wasn't ready,
Because I wasn't brave enough,
Because I wasn't enough.

I hope you found your peace.
I hope you found someone
Who could love you
The way I couldn't.
And if you haven't,
I hope you know—

It was never you.
It was me.

13. The Swan

On a quiet lake, under the soft glow of the moon,
two swans glided across the still water.
Their feathers were white as snow,
their movements smooth, like a gentle song.
They met one evening, hidden among tall reeds,
and in that moment, the world seemed to stop.
Their eyes locked, speaking a language without words,
a silent promise to never part.
From that day, they were always together,
moving as one, side by side.
Their love wasn't loud or showy;
it was simple, steady, and strong.
People say swans stay with one partner for life.
If one calls out, the other hears,
no matter how far they are.
And if one is lost,
the other doesn't look for a new partner—
it waits, carrying the weight of love
like a treasure too precious to replace.
Swans remind us of what love should be:
not about owning, but about sharing.
Not about changing someone,

but accepting them just as they are.
Their beauty isn't just in their white feathers
or their graceful moves,
but in their loyalty—
a promise they keep every single day.
Even when storms come,
and the lake ripples with chaos,
they stay close, protecting each other,
showing us that love isn't just for easy days,
but for the hard ones too.
And when their time on this earth ends,
they sing one last song—
not of sadness, but of thanks.
For a life filled with love,
for every moment spent together.
Swans teach us that love doesn't have to be grand.
It can be quiet, like the soft touch of water.
It can be simple, like a glance that says, "I'm here."
But it must be real,
loyal, and strong enough to last a lifetime.
So, the next time you see a swan,
remember their story.
And ask yourself:
Can we love as they do?
With hearts so pure,
and promises we never break?

14. Extraterrestrial Love

We have no hands,

so we do not touch,

but when I stand beside you,

my antennas tremble,

tuning into the quiet songs of your existence.

We do not have eyes,

so we do not see beauty—

but when you move,

the sky bends around you,

turning the color of first dawn after a hundred eclipses.

We do not have voices,

but when I think of you,

the air between us crackles with unspoken things,

sparks of longing humming between our ribs of stone.

We are not made of flesh,

but of silicon and stardust,

our bodies smooth as the dunes of our violet desert,

our cores pulsing soft like dying suns.

When we love, we glow—

not like fire, but like nebulae,

a slow, swirling bloom of light,

softer than the breath of a comet,

brighter than the birth of a world.
When you are near,
the glow of my body shifts,
my hues melting into yours,
until we are no longer two separate flames
but one great aurora dancing in the dark.
We do not hold each other,
but when the solar winds whisper,
we lean into them,
letting the universe press us close,
as if even the stars wish to keep us entwined.
We do not kiss,
but sometimes, I let my glow flicker,
spelling your name in the silent language of our kind,
watching as you flicker back—
a conversation written in pulses of blue and gold.
When I miss you,
my glow fades to dusk.
When I long for you,
I hum at the frequency of your name,
sending it into the void,
hoping you will hear it in the wind.
When we drift apart,
when the tides pull us to opposite ends of our moonlit world,
I leave a part of my light in your path,
so you will always know
where I have been,

so you will always have a way back to me.
And if one day,
our cores burn out,
if our glow becomes nothing but a distant shimmer,
let it be known—
we loved in light,
and in light, we will always remain.
Even when the last star flickers and dies,
somewhere in the deep,
love will still hum between our abandoned worlds.

15. The Greatest Language

They say the world has thousands of languages,
but the only one no one can master is love.
It has no dictionary,
no grammar,
no rules.
You fumble through it,
inventing your own phrases,
praying the other person
understands your dialect.
It has words you don't say—
the quiet "stay"
hidden in every goodbye,
the unsaid "thank you"
in every sacrifice.
It has punctuation too.
A full stop can end a fight.
An ellipsis can keep it alive.
And don't forget that one misplaced "k"—
it's like putting chilli in chai.
Ruins everything.

But love isn't just in words.
It's in the way
she pulled her hair back
and you thought,
"God must've taken His time with her."
It's in the way
she held your hand once
on a crowded street,
like she wasn't just holding your palm
but anchoring your chaos.
Love speaks in silences,
in sighs shared under starlit skies,
in stolen glances
that say everything
your tongue is too clumsy to articulate.
It's a language
where "I'm fine"
often means "I need you,"
where "good night"
is sometimes a soft cry for "don't let go."
And just when you think
you've mastered it,
love changes the script.
It asks for patience
when you have none,
for forgiveness
when you're drowning in hurt.

It demands fluency
not in words,
but in understanding—
in showing up on the days
you'd rather walk away.
But love is cruel too.
It's the only language
that leaves echoes.
Even in its absence,
it speaks to you.
In the faint scent
of her favourite perfume
lingering on a scarf,
in the sound of a song
you swore you wouldn't listen to again.
It lingers in the empty chair
across the table,
in the unsent messages
you still draft at midnight.
It leaves you with memories
that feel like scars—
not painful,
but permanent.
And yet, love remains.
Even when it's gone,
it sneaks into your sentences,
translates your silence

into a yearning
you didn't ask for.
Because love is more than a language.
It's a mirror
reflecting the best
and worst of you.
It's a firefly
lighting up the darkest nights,
flickering just enough
to remind you
that light exists.
It's a symphony
made of messy notes,
discordant at times,
but somehow it all comes together
when the right person listens.
Love is the only language
that teaches you to unlearn yourself.
To speak less,
but feel more.
And even in its cruelty,
it's beautiful.
Because it's the only language
that needs no translator.
It's heard in a single look.
It's written in the spaces
between "I miss you"

and "I'll always be here."
Honestly,
if love were on Duolingo,
we'd all still be stuck
on Lesson One—
because no one
ever masters the art
of holding another heart.

16. Love of the Heavens

One day, my breath will slow,
my hands will rest,
and my name will fade from daily lips.
But I wonder—
will love remain?
Will it wait for me beyond the Jordan,
where no tear is shed,
where the tree of life spreads its branches wide,
where the New Jerusalem stands,
gates of pearl shining with a light that never fades?
I think of love, not like it is here,
where hands slip away,
where goodbyes are written into every hello,
where time steals even the strongest embrace.
But a love that stays—
a love that was spoken before the foundations of the world,
a love that stretched across Golgotha,
that wept in Gethsemane,
that conquered death on the third day.
In the space between now and forever,
where souls rest in the arms of Abraham,
does love still call my name?

Does it linger in the prayers of the living,
in the mother who still weeps for her lost child,
in the lover who wakes, reaching for someone long gone?
And when the final trumpet sounds,
when the heavens shake,
when the dead rise from their graves,
when the Lamb opens the Book of Life
and every name is spoken once more—
will love still know me?
On that great day,
when the wheat is gathered into the barn
and the chaff is cast to the wind,
when the Shepherd calls His flock by name,
will love be the voice that welcomes me home?
Will it be the hand that lifts me
when my soul is heavy?
And if grace leads me in,
if the gates of Zion open wide,
will I see those I lost,
standing by the river of life,
beside waters too pure for this world?
Will they smile as if no time has passed,
as if sorrow never touched them,
as if love had never been interrupted—
only paused?
Will I drink from the cup of peace,
beneath the tree whose leaves heal the nations?

Will I walk the streets of gold,
where love is not a fleeting moment,
but a kingdom that will never fall?
Love in this world is fragile.
Love in this world is borrowed.
But the love beyond—
the love that was, that is, and that will be—
is written in light,
sealed by the Alpha and the Omega,
carved into eternity itself.
It does not fade.
It does not break.
It simply waits—
beyond the veil.

17. Promises

There was a time
when her eyes mirrored the sky—
bright, endless, full of possibilities.
And in those eyes,
I made a vow,
not spoken in words,
but etched into the marrow of my being.
A promise to bring a change,
to turn grief into hope,
to make people smile
even when the world seemed
bent on bending me.
I swore to her—
that even when the nights grew heavy
and the mornings felt hollow,
my lips would carry a smile,
a shield against the weight of despair.
Now she's gone.
Her laughter lingers only in the cracks of my memory,
a melody I hum to myself
on the days when silence feels unbearable.
But the promise?

The promise is still here,

alive,

staring at me like a ghost in the mirror.

I hear her voice sometimes,

"Promises are not to be broken,

not even by time,

not even by loss."

And I believe her.

Because she knew me better than I knew myself.

She knew I'd carry these vows,

like scars,

like armour,

like a flame that refuses to die

no matter how fierce the storm.

I walk among faces—

strangers,

friends,

souls unknown,

and I wonder:

Can they feel it too?

The weight of her hope resting on my shoulders,

the burden of a love so profound

it demands to be spread like wildfire,

touching lives,

melting sorrows,

building bridges where hearts have cracked.

They call it strength—
this resilience,
this refusal to crumble.
But they don't know it's not mine.
It's hers.
It's the light she left behind,
the fire she kindled
when she said,
"You were born to give,
to heal,
to fight."
I take her words like medicine
on the days when the darkness creeps in.
I remind myself:
This is not just my journey.
It's hers, too.
It's ours,
a promise forged in love,
tested by time,
and unbroken by separation.
Let the world hear me!
Let them see the cracks in my resolve
and watch as I fill them with gold.
Let them know—
that even in her absence,
she is present in every smile I create,
every tear I wipe away,

every moment I stand firm
when the ground beneath me trembles.
I will not break.
I cannot break.
Because I have promised to live for others,
to become a lighthouse
in the storm of their sorrow.
And if I fail,
I fail her.
So let my voice thunder,
let my actions roar louder than words.
I will make the change.
I will carry her dream.
I will smile,
not for myself,
but for the love
that still breathes
in every promise I made to her.

18. The Loveless world

Let me take you there.
Not in stories, not in voices—
but in flesh, in shadow, in the scream
that never leaves your throat.
This is the world after love has died.
Do not look away.
There is nowhere left to run.
The trees do not just shed their leaves—
they vomit them,
ripping their own limbs apart in desperation,
barking out silent wails,
their trunks hollowed like graves
waiting for something to crawl inside.
There is no wind anymore,
only a breath—slow, damp, reeking—
that slithers through the streets,
touching your neck, whispering your name,
though no one is left to say it.
The flowers?
They have not wilted.
They have not died.

They have turned inside out,
their petals curling like flesh in fire,
their veins pulsing—beating—
as if something still lives within them,
something that should not.
The soil is wet but never from rain.
Do not dig.
Do not ask why.
The sun is not a star anymore.
It is an open wound in the sky,
bleeding rust-coloured light,
spilling sickness over the land.
Its heat does not warm,
it only peels—
skin, bark, walls, sanity.
It watches without eyes.
It sees without blinking.
And when it sets,
the real nightmare begins.
The moon—oh, the moon.
Once a lullaby, a poet, a quiet guardian—
now it dangles, cracked and jagged,
a shard of bone in a blackened jaw.
It does not reflect light anymore.
It only swallows it.
And the stars?
They have fled.

The sky is empty,
a vast, endless grave
where even light has chosen to die.
Water does not flow.
It writhes.
Thick, black, bubbling—
it does not carry fish, nor leaves, nor life.
It carries faces, distorted and gasping,
eyes wide, mouths open,
as if still screaming beneath the surface.
Drink, and they will scream inside you.
The wells whisper.
The lakes watch.
The rain never falls,
but sometimes, if you listen,
you can hear it sobbing
from somewhere far, far away.
The hospitals are full,
but no one leaves.
The beds are made,
but no one sleeps.
The doctors still wear white,
but it is not for purity.
It is the colour of bones, of forgotten things,
of hands that no longer save—
only take.

They move in silence,
their scalpels cold, their fingers steady.
The infants do not cry when they are taken.
They never get the chance.
Mothers wake up with empty arms
and no memory of ever holding anything at all.
The streets are lined with bodies,
but no one is dead.
Not fully.
They sit—
on curbs, on sidewalks, on the steps of houses
that have long forgotten their names.
Their mouths do not move.
Their chests do not rise.
But if you step too close,
their heads turn—
slowly, unnaturally,
bones creaking, necks twisting
like wilted flowers reaching for light
that no longer exists.
The children do not play.
Their laughter does not echo.
They stand in doorways,
eyes black as the void,
motionless.
If you blink,
they might be closer.

If you run,
they might follow.
If you ask their names,
they might give you yours instead.
Somewhere, there is a house.
Not yours, not mine,
but familiar—achingly, terribly familiar.
Its windows are open,
but the wind never moves the curtains.
Its door is ajar,
but no one leaves.
Inside, there are no voices.
No footsteps.
Only the sound of something being forgotten.
A mother stands in the kitchen,
stirring a pot filled with nothing.
A father sits in his chair,
reading a newspaper with blank pages.
A lover holds a letter,
but every time they blink,
the words fade,
until there is nothing left
but trembling hands
holding a piece of paper
that means nothing at all.
This is not death.
Death would be a kindness.

SWARN VERMA

This is something worse.
A world without love
is a world without memory,
without warmth, without a reason to wake up,
without a reason to be.
And it is waiting.
Behind your reflection.
Under your bed.
At the edge of sleep,
where dreams rot into nightmares.
Do not let it in.
Do not let it in.

19. Healing Force

turning wounds into sacred scars of healing.
Love for humanity,
not bound by borders, not measured by names.
A love that saw no colour,
no castes, no lines etched in sand.
It was the doctor who stayed
when the world turned away,
the poet who wrote verses
that cradled the broken.
Then love touched the beasts,
the roots, the rivers,
whispered to the mountains,
and kissed the sky.
The earth, long battered,
exhaled in quiet relief.
The birds no longer sang dirges,
and the trees no longer wept resin tears.
And love found God,
not in temples or altars alone,
but in the breath between words,
in the space between heartbeats.
God, who had waited,
not with anger, but with patience.
Love was the prayer that needed no words,
the faith that had no fear.
When hatred finally fell silent,
and love became the only language,

we saw the truth, etched in light:
That love was never weakness,
never a thing to be bartered,
but the only power that could save us.
A child,
born into this world anew,
knew no enemy,
feared no stranger.
For in the end,
when all was said and done,
the only revolution,
the only salvation,
the only miracle,
was love.
And so it spread,
like dawn upon a sleeping world,
tender, golden, insistent,
until the darkness had nowhere left to hide.
Hands met hands, old wounds faded,
and laughter rose where once silence reigned.
Love was the thread that wove humanity together,
and we, at last, remembered
we were always meant to be one.
The oceans, once raging,
softened under the touch of kindness.
The deserts, cracked and barren,
blossomed where love walked.

Even the stones, once cold and unmoving,

could feel the warmth of belonging.

No longer did we name our differences,

no longer did we fear the unknown.

Strangers became family,

and the past, no matter how cruel,

was forgiven in the arms of love.

The moon no longer hung over

fields of battle,

but watched over lovers,

and children who had never known war.

Love became law,

not written on paper,

but etched in every heart.

The judge ruled with mercy,

the leader served with grace,

and power was not sought,

only shared, like the morning sun.

And as the years passed,

no one remembered the time before,

when hatred was currency,

and division was a way of life.

For what was lost,

was never worth keeping,

and what was found,

was everything we had ever needed.

The sky itself,

freed from the burden of sorrow,
burst into colours never seen before.
And the stars, knowing the truth at last,
bowed to the greatest force
that ever was,
that ever will be:
Love.
And in this world reborn,
where no voice trembled in fear,
and no soul carried the weight of yesterday's pain,
love built bridges where walls once stood.
It was in the laughter of children,
in the songs of the old,
in the quiet touch of two hands meeting
without hesitation, without fear.
Love mended the ruins,
not only of shattered cities,
but of shattered hearts.
It whispered through the winds,
and painted hope upon the faces of those
who once believed kindness was a myth.
It flowed through the veins of the earth,
soaking into the roots, blooming in the fields.
No hand was left empty,
no soul was left in the cold.
Love warmed like fire,
not to destroy, but to ignite

SWARN VERMA

something long lost—
the belief that we were all meant to be whole.
And when the final echoes of hatred died,
when there were no more names for war,
and no more reasons for sorrow,
the world stood in stillness,
and love, in all its quiet power,
smiled upon creation,
knowing its work was finally done.
And so it carried on,
like a hymn woven into the wind,
like the murmur of waves upon a forgiving shore.
It was found in the hush of twilight,
in the promise of dawn,
in every embrace that said,
"You are home."
Love endured,
not as a fleeting dream,
but as the essence of life itself.
For as long as hearts beat,
as long as hands reached,
as long as eyes met with kindness,
love would remain—
unbroken, unwavering,
and eternal.

20. Why agent of love ?

the quiet, eternal truth about love.
Love isn't a fleeting moment.
It isn't the grand confessions
or the fireworks we've been taught to expect.
Love is an ocean, vast and steady,
its waves touching shores
it'll never claim as its own.
I became a seeker,
an observer of this infinite ocean.
I noticed how love thrives
in the simplest acts—
a stranger offering their seat to an elder,
a mother braiding her daughter's hair,
a gardener planting a tree ,
the fruits of which he might never see .
Love, I realised, is not something you take.
It is something you become.
But becoming love is not easy.
It demands that you unlearn
everything you thought you knew.
It asks for your ego,
your pride,
your need for control.
It demands sacrifice—
not of wealth or power,
but of the walls you've built
to keep yourself safe.

Because to truly love
is to risk being vulnerable.
And vulnerability is terrifying.
It's like standing in the rain,
knowing you might catch a cold,
but also knowing
the rain will wash you clean.
Love is not a transaction.
It is not, "I give you this, so you give me that."
Love is giving without the need to receive.
It is the light of a diya,
burning simply because it must.
I began to see myself differently.
I was no longer someone in love,
but someone of love.
And with that shift,
the world changed.
The pain of loss didn't vanish—
it transformed.
What was once a wound
became a window.
Through it, I saw the beauty
in other people's stories.
I saw the young man holding his father's hand,
walking slower than he wanted to.
I saw the teacher staying late,
just to make sure her weakest student understood.

I saw the shopkeeper smiling,
even after a long, thankless day.
And I thought,
"This is love.
This is what it looks like
when you stop expecting
and start giving."
I gave myself a name—
not for glory,
but for purpose.
Agent of Love.
Because the world doesn't need more critics.
It doesn't need more walls,
or more reasons to divide.
What the world needs
is connection,
understanding,
and love that asks for nothing in return.
So I began my journey.
Not to preach,
but to practice.
To remind myself, every day,
that love is not an emotion—
it is a choice.
It is the choice to forgive
when anger feels easier.
It is the choice to listen

when silence feels safer.
It is the choice to hold on
when letting go feels like relief.
Love is not for the faint-hearted.
It will test you,
break you,
and rebuild you.
But in the end,
it is the only thing worth being.
And so I walk this path,
not as someone who has mastered love,
but as someone who is learning,
every single day.
I don't know where this journey will take me.
I don't know if it will heal
all the wounds I carry.
But I know this:
Love is not something you wait for.
It is something you become.
And that, my friends,
is why I write
under the pen name of —
"Agent of love"

"A hundred poems in a hundred days.

This journey wouldn't have been the same without **Sahityika, the literary society of IIT Madras BS degree**. *Their encouragement and unwavering support made every word feel heard.*

To every reader who has turned these pages, felt these verses, and carried them forward—thank you.

—Swarn Verma"